TO...

C000009028

I PROMISE...

... TO GO FOR A BIKE RIDE WITH YOU.

SIGNED... DATE.........................

YOU'RE THE BEST

TO..

I PROMISE...

... TO GIVE YOU
CONTROL OF THE
REMOTE ALL DAY.

SIGNED.. DATE.........................

YOU'RE THE BEST

TO...

I PROMISE...

... TO LISTEN TO ONE OF YOUR FAVOURITE ALBUMS WITH YOU AND TO TURN THE VOLUME UP LOUD.

SIGNED.. DATE........................

YOU'RE THE BEST

TO...

I PROMISE...

... TO MAKE YOUR
SANDWICHES FOR
A WHOLE WEEK.

SIGNED.. DATE.........................

YOU'RE THE BEST

TO...

I PROMISE...

... TO SPEND A DAY WITH
YOU, DOING SOMETHING
YOU REALLY LOVE.

SIGNED.. DATE..........................

YOU'RE THE BEST

TO...

I PROMISE...

... TO LISTEN TO YOU
TALK ABOUT YOUR
CHILDHOOD MEMORIES.

SIGNED.. DATE.......................

YOU'RE THE BEST

TO..

I PROMISE...

... TO DO THE
WASHING-UP EVERY
DAY FOR A WEEK.

SIGNED... DATE..........................

YOU'RE THE BEST

TO...

I PROMISE...

... TO LAUGH AT ALL YOUR
DAD JOKES (ESPECIALLY
IF THEY'RE TERRIBLE).

SIGNED... DATE.....................

YOU'RE THE BEST

TO...

I PROMISE...

... TO HELP COOK
YOUR FAVOURITE
DINNER FOR YOU.

SIGNED... DATE........................

YOU'RE THE BEST

TO...

I PROMISE...

... TO WATCH
YOUR FAVOURITE
SPORT WITH YOU.

SIGNED.. DATE.........................

YOU'RE THE BEST

TO...

I PROMISE...

... TO GO CAMPING
WITH YOU AT
THE WEEKEND.

SIGNED..   DATE............................

YOU'RE THE BEST

TO..

I PROMISE...

... TO TAKE THE BINS OUT FOR YOU.

SIGNED.. DATE..........................

YOU'RE THE BEST

TO...

I PROMISE...

... TO WATCH YOUR
FAVOURITE FILM
WITH YOU.

SIGNED.. DATE........................

YOU'RE THE BEST

TO...

I PROMISE...

... TO SPEND AN AFTERNOON IN YOUR COMPANY, OFF MY GADGETS.

SIGNED... DATE.........................

YOU'RE THE BEST

TO..

I PROMISE...

... TO MAKE A PLAYLIST OF OUR FAVOURITE SONGS.

SIGNED... DATE..........................

YOU'RE THE BEST

TO..

I PROMISE...

... TO LEARN SOMETHING
NEW WITH YOU.

SIGNED... DATE...........................

YOU'RE THE BEST

TO...

I PROMISE...

... TO HAVE A GOOD OLD TRADITIONAL GAMES AFTERNOON WITH YOU.

SIGNED... DATE...........................

YOU'RE THE BEST

TO..

I PROMISE...

**... TO LET YOU TEACH
ME ALL ABOUT DIY
(AND TO BE CAREFUL
WITH YOUR TOOLS).**

SIGNED...   DATE.........................

YOU'RE THE BEST

TO..

I PROMISE...

... NOT TO TELL ANYONE
NEXT TIME YOU GET
A TAKEAWAY INSTEAD
OF COOKING.

SIGNED.. DATE.........................

YOU'RE THE BEST

TO...

I PROMISE...

... TO HELP YOU
WASH YOUR CAR.

SIGNED.. DATE................................

YOU'RE THE BEST

TO...

I PROMISE...

... TO MAKE
YOU PROUD.

SIGNED...   DATE........................

YOU'RE THE BEST

TO..

I PROMISE...

... TO TIDY
YOUR SHED.

SIGNED.. DATE..........................

YOU'RE THE BEST

TO..

I PROMISE...

... TO HELP YOU CUT
THE GRASS, OR TO
DO IT FOR YOU.

SIGNED.. DATE.......................

YOU'RE THE BEST

TO...

I PROMISE...

... TO SHOW
YOU RESPECT.

SIGNED.. DATE....................

YOU'RE THE BEST

TO..

I PROMISE...

... TO MAKE YOU A CUP OF TEA (OR COFFEE) JUST THE WAY YOU LIKE IT.

SIGNED.. DATE.........................

YOU'RE THE BEST

TO...

I PROMISE...

... TO MAKE MY BED
AND YOUR BED EVERY
DAY FOR A WEEK.

SIGNED.. DATE.........................

YOU'RE THE BEST

TO...

I PROMISE...

... TO CREATE A PHOTO-
MONTAGE WITH YOU OF
SOME OF OUR FAVOURITE
TIMES TOGETHER.

SIGNED.. DATE.....................

YOU'RE THE BEST

TO..

I PROMISE...

... TO DO MY CHORES
WITHOUT YOU
HAVING TO ASK.

SIGNED...   DATE........................

YOU'RE THE BEST

TO...

I PROMISE...

... TO TRY A NEW
SPORT WITH YOU.

SIGNED... DATE...............................

YOU'RE THE BEST

TO...

I PROMISE...

... TO EAT ALL MY DINNER.

SIGNED.. DATE.........................

YOU'RE THE BEST

TO..

I PROMISE...

... TO TRY MY BEST
IN WHATEVER YOU
ASK ME TO DO.

SIGNED.. DATE.........................

YOU'RE THE BEST

TO..

... TO GO ON
AN ADVENTURE
WITH YOU.

SIGNED.. DATE.......................

YOU'RE THE BEST